DRASTIC PLASTIC & TROUBLESOME TRASH

CARLTON KIDS

THIS IS A CARLTON BOOK

Published in 2019 by Carlton Books Limited,
an imprint of the Carlton Publishing Group,
20 Mortimer Street, London W1T 3JW

A catalogue record for this book is available from
the British Library.

ISBN: 978-1-78312-479-4

Printed in Dongguan, China

10 9 8 7 6 5 4 3 2 1

FSC
MIX
Paper
FSC® C144853

Executive Editor: Bryony Davies
Design Manager: Emily Clarke
Designer: Darren Jordan
Production: Nicola Davey

The publishers would like to thank the following
sources for their kind permission to reproduce
the pictures in this book. Key: T=top, B=bottom,
L=left, R=right, C=centre, BKG=background

Alamy Stock Photo: /PhotoAlto sas: 27C

Shutterstock: /Africa Studio: 35L, 40-41BKG,
41TL; /Aleksandra Suzi: 57BL, 57BR; /AlenKadr:
25TR; /AlexandrBognat: 57TR; /Alf Manciagli:
44-45; /alfocome: 21TR; /Amberside: 17L; /anek.
soowannaphoom: 33BL; /antb: 60R; /Aphelleon:
4-5BKG; /arikbintang: 55BL; /Arnon.ap: 24-25BKG; /
asliozber: 17R; /azure: 59L; /Berka7: 32-33BKG; /
Bessarab: 18BR, 34C, 42L; /Big Foot Productions:
4CB, 23BR; /BravissimoS: 58BL; /Chaikom: 5T; /
CHAIWATPHOTOS: 4B; /Chaiwuth Wichitdho: 60BL;
/Chocosummer: 43TL; /Christopher Boswell: 26-
27BKG; /Dalibor Danilovic: 8-9BKG; /DAMRONG
RATTANAPONG: 42BC; /Dario Lo Presti: 36-37BKG; /
Dmitry Rukhlenko: 22-23BKG; /Dmytro Zinkevych: 61R;
/donatas1205: 20C; /Dragan Milovanovic: 15B; /Elena
Elisseeva: 55TR; /Ethan Daniels: 13BR; /Evan Lorne:
56-57BKG, 57R; /Evannovostro: 47BR; /exopixel: 35C;
/FabrikaSimf: 34R, 39R; /foxhound photos: 58TC; /
girl-think-position: 26BR; /gloverk: 25BR; /Guitar
photographer: 55BR; /HelloRF Zcool: 18BL; /Huguette
Roe: 10-11BKG; /Jag_cz: 20-21BKG; /K. D. P.: 42-
43BKG; /kamilpetran: 38-39BKG; /kanusommer: 35TC;
/kc look: 9B; /Kenishirotie: 41BR; /Kira Garmashova:
47R; /Kletr: 28-29BKG; /Kokhanchikov: 31BR; /Koxae
Sun: 43L; /Leonid Ikan: 46-47BKG; /LightField Studios:
50TC; /Luminis: 51TR; /M. Unal Ozmen: 25BC; /
macrowildlife: 37C; /Magdalena Kucova: 27R; /marcin
jucha: 58BC; /Mariyana M: 25BL, 26BL; /Makistock:
18L; /Marius GODOI: 51C; /mbrphoto: 50R; /Meister
Photos: 35TR; /Menna: 35TL; /MidoSemsem: 18TR; /
Minoru K: 5CB, 52-53; /MOAimage: 42BL; /Mohamed
Abdulraheem: 6-7BKG; /Mouse family: 34BC; /
nelzajamal: 54-55BKG; /Neophuket: 55TL; /ninefera:
27L; /Oleksandr_Delyk: 49BL; /Olga Gorevan: 60-
61BKG; /Olga Vasilyeva: 31C; /onair: 26TL; /phive:
15T; /phomphan: 49TL; /photka: 51L, 59C; /Picsfive:
49BR; /pjhpix: 34-35BKG; /POTILA MR.PHANTONG:
43TR; /pratan ounpitipong: 25TL; /Protasov AN: 26TR;
/Rawpixel.com: 5B, 15R; /Rich Carey: 4CT, 12-13BKG;
/robert_s: 6B; /Rose Seyfried: 50C; /RusGri: 33BR;
/samritk: 33TR; /Sanit Fuangnakhon: 5CT, 18TC; /
Sergey Peterman: 34TC; /Sergey Uryadnikov: 29T;
/SHTRAUS DMYTRO: 39L; /sibadan: 50-51BKG; /
Somchai Som: 33TL; /Sophie McAulay: 59TL; /
Subbotina Anna: 30-31BKG; /SUE WETJEN: 50BC; /
Surkov Vladimir: 61L; /Surrphoto: 47TL; /Sutthimon
Ounnapiruk: 42BR; /Suzanne Tucker: 11B; /Svetoslav
Radkov: 58TL; /T photography: 39BR; /tamara321:
51TL; /ThamKC: 17BR; /Tommy Lee Walker: 59TC; /
traveladdict: 43R; /ugurv: 34L; /vchal: 4T; /Versta:
18TL; /vipman: 50L; /Willyam Bradberry: 1BKG,
2-3BKG; /Zu Kamilov: 58C

Every effort has been made to acknowledge
correctly and contact the source and/or copyright
holder of each picture and Carlton Books Limited
apologises for any unintentional errors or
omissions that will be corrected in future editions
of this book.

DRASTIC PLASTIC & TROUBLESOME TRASH

Written by Hannah Wilson

CARLTON KIDS

CONTENTS

TRASHING THE PLANET

What can you see around you? Plastic toys, an odd sock, a paper? All this stuff is piling up, turning our planet into a rubbish heap. The way we make, use and throw away things harms Earth, but we're going to do something about it. Let's investigate plastic, paper, glass, metal, cloth and food and stop them trashing the planet.

HUMANS PRODUCE 40 BILLION TONNES OF CARBON DIOXIDE EVERY YEAR.

CARBON FOOTPRINTS

A carbon footprint measures the amount of carbon dioxide (and other greenhouse gases) produced by an object or activity. For example, the carbon footprint of a sock includes the carbon dioxide (CO_2) released by growing cotton, making the cloth inside a factory and transporting it to the shops.

CO_2 wraps around our planet and, just like a greenhouse, lets the Sun's heat in but not out. As Earth warms, the climate changes. Ice caps melt, which raises sea levels, and droughts, floods and wildfires destroy the homes of people and animals.

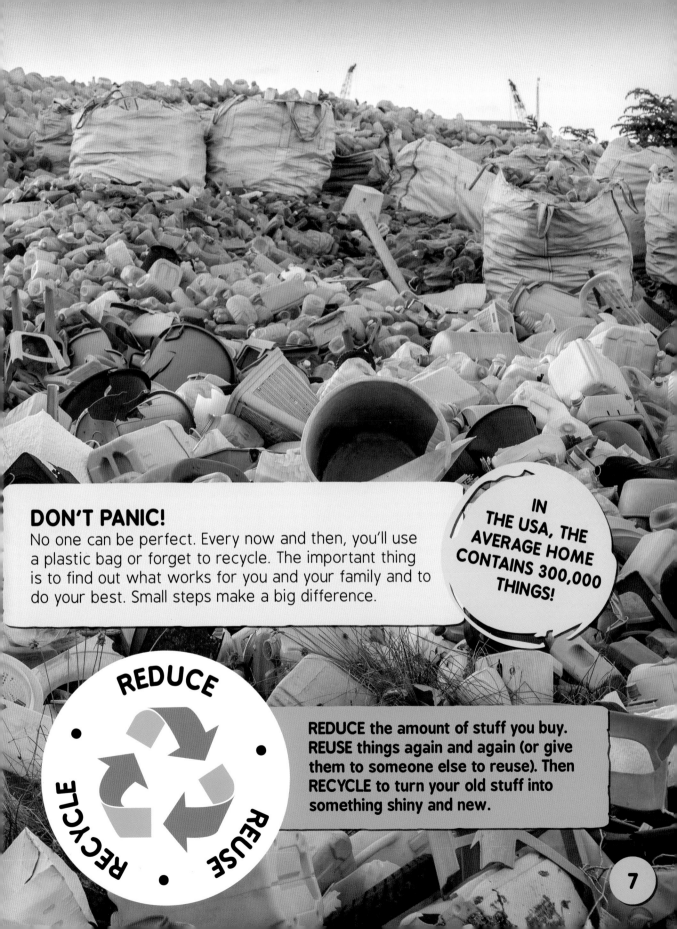

DON'T PANIC!
No one can be perfect. Every now and then, you'll use a plastic bag or forget to recycle. The important thing is to find out what works for you and your family and to do your best. Small steps make a big difference.

IN THE USA, THE AVERAGE HOME CONTAINS 300,000 THINGS!

REDUCE

RECYCLE

REUSE

REDUCE the amount of stuff you buy. REUSE things again and again (or give them to someone else to reuse). Then RECYCLE to turn your old stuff into something shiny and new.

LOADS OF LANDFILL

Every year, we humans throw billions of tonnes of rubbish in the bin. It's taken away by trucks, dumped in huge pits and (usually) buried. This is landfill. Hold your noses — we're going in!

METHANE

As landfill waste decomposes (breaks down), toxic gases such as ammonia are produced, polluting the air. The most harmful gas, created deep within those rotting piles of trash where there is little or no oxygen, is methane. It's not toxic, but it is a greenhouse gas 25 times more powerful than carbon dioxide.

BURN OR BURY?

When space is limited, trash is often incinerated (destroyed by burning), rather than put in landfill. Although the heat produced can be used to make electricity, normal power stations use less energy to do that. Burning landfill can also pump out harmful gases, and burning it in this way may make us feel we don't have to try so hard to recycle.

CHEMICAL SOUP

When rainwater seeps through landfill, it can absorb toxic chemicals such as lead, arsenic and mercury. The polluted water, called leachate, washes into soil and underground water supplies. Some landfill sites have waterproof linings to stop this. The leachate is collected and cleaned. But the process isn't perfect — the linings can leak and the cleaning process uses a great deal of energy.

✗ TIP ✗

All the plastic toothbrushes you've ever used are probably lying in landfill. They'll be there for hundreds of years. Try a bamboo toothbrush instead – it will biodegrade (rot away).

THE WORLD'S LARGEST LANDFILLS CAN COVER AN AREA THE SIZE OF 1,000 FOOTBALL PITCHES AND RECEIVE 10,000 TONNES OF TRASH EVERY DAY.

RECYCLING CENTRE

Recycling turns old into new and uses less energy than making stuff from scratch. Always squash, crush and flatten your recycling – if it takes up less space, fewer petrol-guzzling trucks are needed to transport it.

SUPER SORTING

We'll soon find out how new things are made from plastic, paper, glass and metal. But how are those materials separated from each other at recycling centres?

1 Workers pick out plastic bags, clothing and other items that will be landfilled or recycled separately.

2 An 'air knife' blows light paper and cardboard up a huge duct on to another conveyor belt.

4 Magnets extract steel cans, and an 'eddy current' creates a magnetic force to push aluminium on to another conveyor belt.

3 Pieces of heavy glass fall into separate bins.

5 Lasers or special cameras identify different types of plastic. Blasts of air push them into different containers.

6 The separated materials are squashed into huge bales, ready for transportation to specialist recycling centres.

THREE REASONS TO RECYCLE

1. Making things with stuff we already have means we don't need to dig up oil to make plastic or chop down trees for paper. This saves Earth's natural resources and protects green spaces.

2. Recycling saves energy because fewer fossil fuels are needed to make things with existing materials. This means less greenhouse gas is released.

3. If we recycle, less stuff will be landfilled, incinerated or littered.

ONE TONNE OF RECYCLED PLASTICS SAVES ABOUT 16 BARRELS OF OIL AND LANDFILL SPACE THE SIZE OF A MINIBUS.

✗ TIP ✗

This book is full of recycling tips, but your local area may have some different rules. Ask an adult to help you find out what to put in your recycling bin and what to take to a local waste centre.

Mixed materials are harder to recycle. Cartons are made of card with a plastic or aluminium foil lining. They can probably go in your recycling bin (squashed, with straws pushed inside or lids screwed on). Things like toasters are crushed so that the small pieces of plastic and metal can be sorted.

PLASTIC

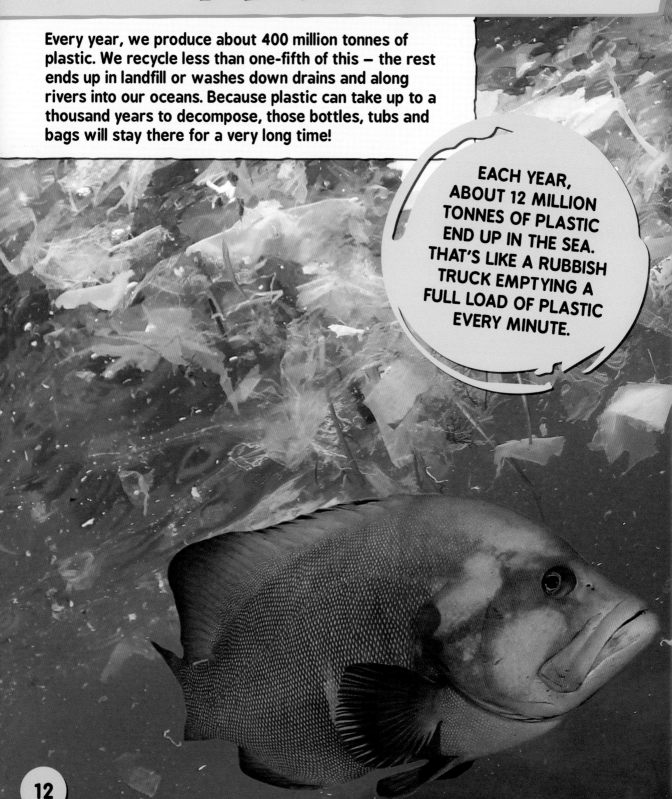

Every year, we produce about 400 million tonnes of plastic. We recycle less than one-fifth of this – the rest ends up in landfill or washes down drains and along rivers into our oceans. Because plastic can take up to a thousand years to decompose, those bottles, tubs and bags will stay there for a very long time!

EACH YEAR, ABOUT 12 MILLION TONNES OF PLASTIC END UP IN THE SEA. THAT'S LIKE A RUBBISH TRUCK EMPTYING A FULL LOAD OF PLASTIC EVERY MINUTE.

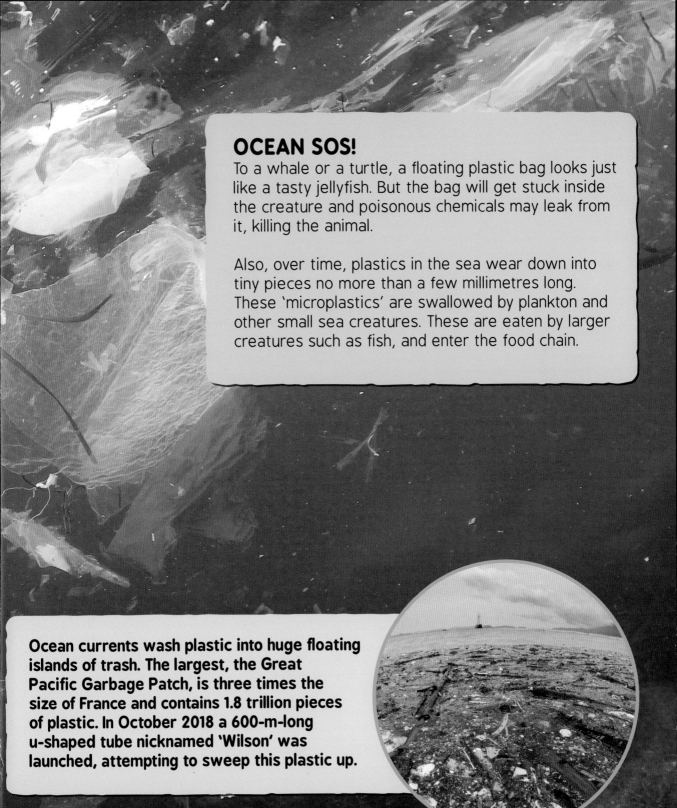

OCEAN SOS!

To a whale or a turtle, a floating plastic bag looks just like a tasty jellyfish. But the bag will get stuck inside the creature and poisonous chemicals may leak from it, killing the animal.

Also, over time, plastics in the sea wear down into tiny pieces no more than a few millimetres long. These 'microplastics' are swallowed by plankton and other small sea creatures. These are eaten by larger creatures such as fish, and enter the food chain.

Ocean currents wash plastic into huge floating islands of trash. The largest, the Great Pacific Garbage Patch, is three times the size of France and contains 1.8 trillion pieces of plastic. In October 2018 a 600-m-long u-shaped tube nicknamed 'Wilson' was launched, attempting to sweep this plastic up.

MAKING PLASTIC

Plastic is a strong, light material that can be moulded into almost any shape, from a hard plastic bowl or thin sheet of cling film to a stretchy pair of socks. If plastic piles up, it pollutes our planet. But the problems begin even before you throw plastic away...

PLASTIC FACTORY

1 Crude oil is heated. Oil contains carbon and releases harmful CO_2 when heated. CO_2 is also released when fuel is burnt or electricity is created to heat the oil.

3 Colourful dyes are added, along with chemicals to make the mixture stretchy or flame-resistant.

CO_2

2 Gases from the boiling oil condense to form hydrocarbons.

4 The mixture is formed into pellets. The pellets are (re)melted...

...then poured into a mould to make a bowl...

...or squeezed through rollers to make cling film...

...or forced through a sieve with tiny holes to make fibres to weave into socks.

CO_2 CO_2 CO_2 CO_2

PLASTIC CARS AND PLANES

It's not just toy vehicles that are made of plastic – real-life cars and planes can be up to 50 per cent plastic. This makes them light, which means they need less fuel. So, plastic *can* be energy-saving. We just need to find planet-friendly ways to make it and dispose of it.

Car tyres are made mostly of synthetic (human-made) rubber – a type of stretchy plastic. Tiny bits of plastic rub off on roads and are washed down drains.

TOTALLY TRUE - OR - FOOLISHLY FALSE?

☐ Up to 700,000 plastic microfibres are released from polyester or nylon clothes during a single washing cycle.

☐ Microplastics are too big to slip through filters in underground drains, so they never wash into our rivers and oceans.

Answers are at the back of the book.

RECYCLING PLASTIC

In the UK, about 38.5 million plastic bottles are used every day, and 16 million of these are not recycled! They end up as litter, in landfill or being destroyed by burning, which produces 233,000 tonnes of CO_2.

HOW A PLASTIC BOTTLE IS RECYCLED INTO A... PLASTIC BOTTLE!

1 Bottles are sorted into different types, then squashed into bales.

2 Plastic degrades (gets worse) with every recycle. It can only be recycled three or four times.

3 Washing removes labels and any leftover liquids.

6 The pellets are melted and made into new products such as carpets, toothbrushes – or bottles!

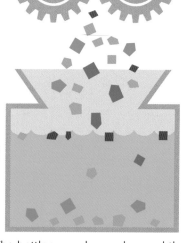

5 The plastic pieces are heated into a hot, gooey liquid and shaped into strands. When the strands have cooled and hardened, they're sliced into pellets.

4 The bottles are chopped up and the pieces are separated in a water tank – some plastics will float (including cap pieces), while others won't.

16

SPOT THE PLASTIC

Look for these symbols on plastic bottles to work out whether they can be recycled.

PET
(Polyethylene terephthalate) Clear drink bottles. Recyclable.

HDPE
(High-density polyethylene) Bottles for milk and shampoo. Recyclable.

PVC
(Polyvinyl chloride) Large squash bottles, cooking oil bottles. Not always recyclable.

PP
(Polypropylene) Ketchup bottles and bottle caps. Not always recyclable.

TIP

For advice on recycling tricky plastics, look at the recycling pages of your local council's website, or check out recyclenow.com.

RECYCLING TIPS

There are lots of things you can do to help cut down plastic waste.

 Empty and rinse before recycling. Liquids can damage recycling machinery or other recyclables.

 Crush your bottles so they take up less space. This means fewer recycling trucks on the road, pumping out CO_2.

 Keep lids on to help the bottles stay crushed. They'll be recycled separately.

Make an eco brick by stuffing non-recyclables into a plastic bottle. This 'brick' can be used as a building material.

PLASTIC FANTASTIC?

Try to avoid single-use plastics – plastic items you use only once. Can you reuse or upcycle that bottle or tray?

REDUCE AND REUSE

Making a plastic bottle and recycling it both use energy and materials. It's even better to reduce and reuse.

✓ Carry your own water bottle.

✓ Use paper straws or simply sip from the side!

✓ Take your own reusable bags when you go shopping.

✓ Soap up with a solid soap bar.

✓ Donate your old toys to a charity shop.

✓ Bring your own tubs for takeaway food.

✓ Try to avoid polyester clothing or check out special washing-machine bags that collect plastic microfibres.

In 2016, 385,000 people signed a petition that successfully persuaded the UK government to ban microbeads in toiletries. People power!

DIY UPCYCLING!

Try these cool crafts to transform your plastic bottles and tubs. Can you think of anything else to make?

A PIGGY BANK

Cut a slot in the back for coins.

A MODEL AEROPLANE

Use painted toilet rolls for jets.

A PEN HOLDER

Glue or tape on a zip from old clothing.

A SELF-WATERING PLANTER

This plant will look after itself.

A BIRD FEEDER

Feed wildlife with bottles and wooden spoons.

TIP

Clean plastic bottles, pots and trays make great bath toys for a small child!

ARE YOU A PROFESSOR OF PLASTICS?

Test your knowledge...

1. How long does plastic take to biodegrade?

- **A.** Up to 10 years
- **B.** Up to 100 years
- **C.** Up to 1,000 years

2. Plastic is mostly made from...

- **A.** Coal
- **B.** Oil
- **C.** Seaweed

3. Plastic can be recycled...

- **A.** 3 to 4 times
- **B.** 30 to 40 times
- **C.** Endlessly

Answers are at the back of the book.

GLASS

Glass is great! We can peer through glass windows and spectacles, drink from glass cups and bottles, and use glass to make greenhouses, jam jars, telescopes and computers. It lasts a very long time, so it must be disposed of properly, but the good news is, glass can be recycled endlessly.

SAFE ON THE SEAFLOOR?

Unlike plastic, glass does not release toxic chemicals that smell good to sea creatures. This means it is less likely to be mistaken for food and eaten by a turtle or whale. Heavy and brittle, glass will break into small lumps and sink to the seafloor, so whales and dolphins can't get stuck in it they way they can in plastic waste.

IT CAN TAKE A MILLION YEARS FOR GLASS TO DECOMPOSE!

SEA GLASS

Tumbling about in the ocean, knocking against rocks and sand, glass breaks into smaller and smaller pieces and is eventually smoothed into pebbles. Look out for colourful 'sea glass' next time you're at the beach!

MAKING GLASS

Glass may not cause as much harm to the oceans as plastic, but the way it is produced can still damage our planet. Huge sand mines and energy-guzzling factories create the glasses you drink from every day.

GLASS FACTORY

Glass is made by heating sand and a few other ingredients, including cullet (crushed-up waste glass). The more cullet that is added, the less energy the process of making new glass requires.

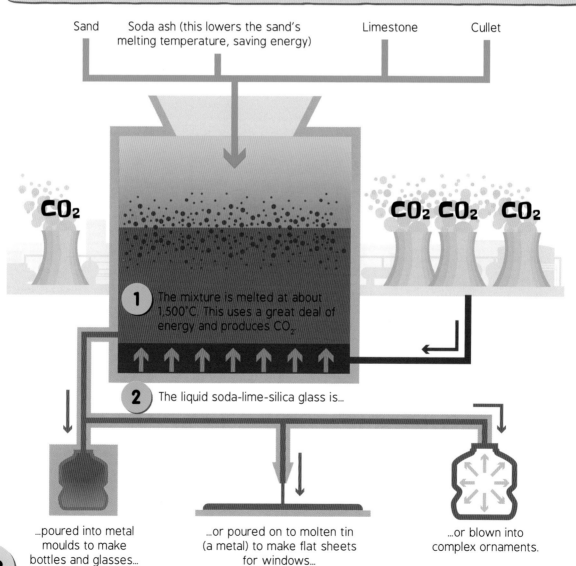

Sand

Soda ash (this lowers the sand's melting temperature, saving energy)

Limestone

Cullet

CO_2

CO_2 CO_2 CO_2

1 The mixture is melted at about 1,500°C. This uses a great deal of energy and produces CO_2.

2 The liquid soda-lime-silica glass is...

...poured into metal moulds to make bottles and glasses...

...or poured on to molten tin (a metal) to make flat sheets for windows...

...or blown into complex ornaments.

SAND MINING

The white silica sand used to make glass is scooped up from beaches by huge diggers, or sucked up pipes from river and ocean beds. This sand mining erodes coastlines and destroys wildlife habitats. If more cullet is used in glass-making, less new sand needs to be mined – so get recycling!

ABOUT 20 BILLION TONNES OF SAND IS MINED EVERY YEAR TO MAKE GLASS, CONCRETE AND OTHER BUILDING MATERIALS.

TOTALLY TRUE - OR - FOOLISHLY FALSE?

Some sand is mined illegally – sand thieves once stole an entire beach in a single night!

Glass is made with sand and cullet, which is crushed-up waste metal.

Answers are at the back of the book.

RECYCLING GLASS

About one-third of glass in the UK is not recycled. That's thousands of tonnes of it littering our landscape instead of being turned into cullet! But why is crushed-up glass from our recycling bins and bottle banks so important? Cullet saves CO_2, keeping our planet cool!

HOW GLASS IS RECYCLED INTO... CULLET!

1 Metal items, such as jar lids and bottle caps, are removed with magnets.

2 Plastic caps and loose bits of paper are sucked up.

3 The glass is washed in hot water to soak away leftover food, liquids or labels.

4 Lasers sort the glass into different colours.

5 The glass is crushed to form cullet, which may be a fine powder or chunks the size of marbles. The cullet is sent off to be re-melted for new glass products, including concrete, tiles and fibreglass insulation for homes, not just bottles.

RECYCLING TIPS

You should be able to recycle all glass used for packaging food and drink. For other items, check the labels for symbols that indicate the glass can be recycled:

 Rinse glass containers – leftover liquids or food can damage other recyclables, such as paper.

 Keep lids on – they will be separated and recycled later.

WHY CAN'T GLASSES BE RECYCLED?

Drinking glasses and heatproof glass oven dishes contain chemicals that cause the glass to melt at different temperatures to jam jars and glass bottles. They wouldn't mix in properly with the recycled liquid glass, spoiling the process.

EVERY TONNE OF GLASS THAT IS RECYCLED INTO NEW GLASS PREVENTS ABOUT 300 KG OF CO_2 BEING RELEASED.

CLASSY GLASS

Before you recycle your glass, try upcycling. Look for jars with unusual shapes or bottles that are bright blue. Whatever you make, place your masterpiece on a sunny windowsill or in front of a lamp and let it light up your life!

REDUCE AND REUSE

Recycling glass is great, but it still uses energy.
Reduce how much you buy and reuse what you have.

✓ Donate old spectacles – some opticians collect them.

✓ Give unwanted drinking glasses to charity.

✓ Fill glass bottles with water and keep them in the fridge.

✓ Empty jam jars make great drinking glasses.

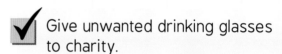

One person's trash is another person's treasure! Support recycling by buying recycled products. Look out for drinking glasses made from 100% recycled glass.

DIY UPCYCLING!

Glass is a beautiful material that can throw light around your room. But don't throw glass around the room – it breaks easily, so be careful!

BE CRAFTY AND USE STUFF FROM INSIDE YOUR HOME – DON'T BUY ANYTHING NEW!

SUPERCOOL STORAGE

MAKE YOUR OWN JAM

A TEA-LIGHT HOLDER

Cut scraps of old cloth to wrap over the lid.

Paint your jars bright colours.

Flames are dangerous – ask an adult to handle the candle!

ARE YOU A GLASS GEEK?
Test your knowledge...

1. Glass takes this long to decompose...

- **A.** 10 years
- **B.** A million years
- **C.** 50,000 years

2. Cullet is...

- **A.** Crushed up waste glass
- **B.** Sea-worn glass pebbles
- **C.** A fish related to a mullet

3. Glass can be recycled...

- **A.** 1 to 2 times
- **B.** 10 to 20 times
- **C.** Endlessly

Answers are at the back of the book.

PAPER

We're diving into a digital world, but paper and cardboard still surround us — from the pages of this book, to shopping receipts, shoe boxes and birthday cards. The good news is that paper biodegrades (rots) and it recycles well. For the bad news, we need to take a trip to the forest...

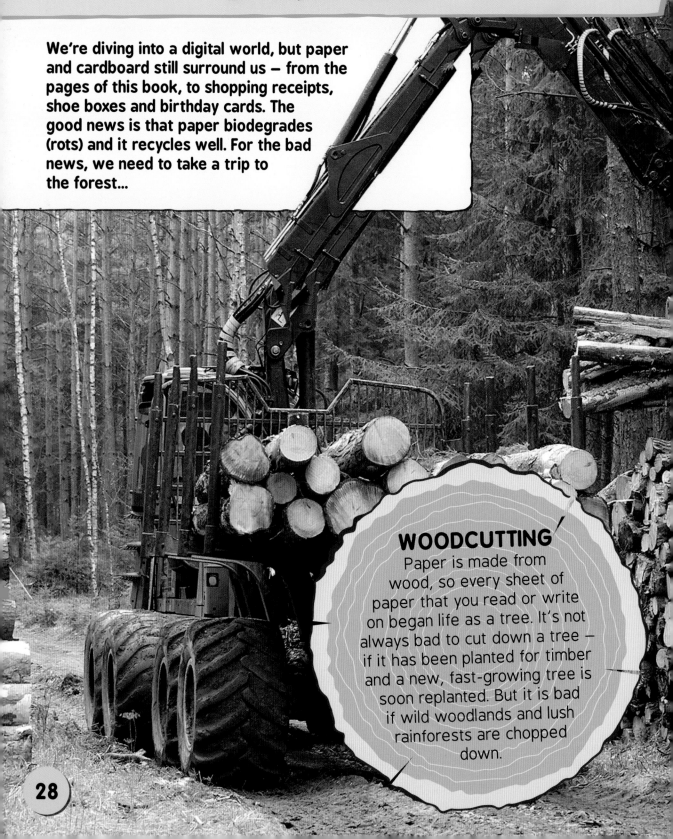

WOODCUTTING

Paper is made from wood, so every sheet of paper that you read or write on began life as a tree. It's not always bad to cut down a tree — if it has been planted for timber and a new, fast-growing tree is soon replanted. But it is bad if wild woodlands and lush rainforests are chopped down.

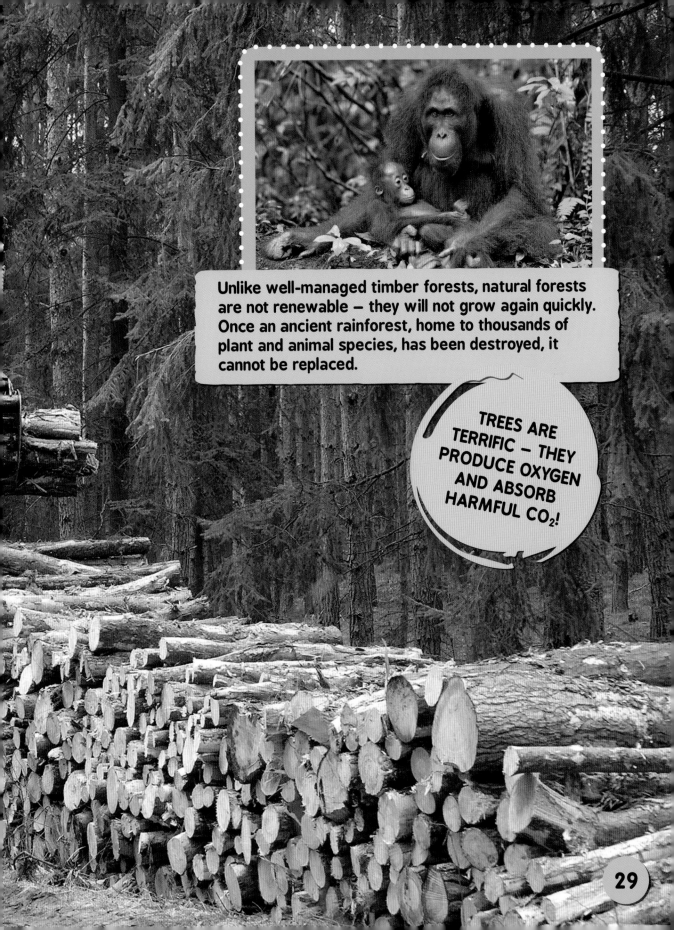

Unlike well-managed timber forests, natural forests are not renewable — they will not grow again quickly. Once an ancient rainforest, home to thousands of plant and animal species, has been destroyed, it cannot be replaced.

TREES ARE TERRIFIC — THEY PRODUCE OXYGEN AND ABSORB HARMFUL CO_2!

MAKING PAPER

Paper is a flattened, dried sheet of mushed-up fibres (strands) of wood. Paper-making is not a perfect process – the factory uses lots of energy and puffs out harmful gases. Chemicals and inks are added to paper, and these will seep into soil and water if the newspaper or greeting card ends up as litter or in landfill.

AT THE PAPER MILL

Trees are pulped to make paper. Leftover bark is often used as a fuel to heat the pulp, saving some energy.

1 Cutters strip away bark from rotating logs.

2 A wood chipper cuts the logs into small pieces.

4 Bleach is poured in to whiten the pulp. Waste bark is used as a fuel to heat the pulp.

3 The wood chips are 'cooked' into a mushy pulp in a tank of hot water.

5 Other chemicals are added for strength.

6 Rollers squeeze out the water and flatten the paste.

7 The paste dries to form paper.

IT TAKES 10 LITRES OF WATER TO MAKE ONE A4 SHEET OF PAPER!

PAPER PICNIC?

A paper napkin takes about four weeks to decompose, while paper plates could take five years because they are often coated in a layer of wax, oil or even plastic. So if you fancy a picnic, take reusable plates from home or check out bamboo plates, which are reusable and biodegradable. Perfect!

Bamboo can be pulped to make plates and cups, clothes and even paper! Whole houses can be built with its strong woody stems. Bamboo is a good green choice — it can grow up to one metre in 24 hours (without chemical fertilisers) and it doesn't need replanting.

WHEN PAPER ROTS, IT RELEASES THE GAS METHANE, WHICH IS 25 TIMES MORE POWERFUL THAN CO_2 AT TRAPPING HEAT ON OUR PLANET!

TOTALLY TRUE - OR - FOOLISHLY FALSE?

☐ A toxic gas called sulphur dioxide is often released from paper factories, and this causes acid rain.

☐ Wood pulp is painted with white paint.

Answers are at the back of the book.

RECYCLING PAPER

Recycling paper saves energy that would have been used to grow and chop down new trees. And it reduces landfill, where paper can take years to decompose.

HOW PAPER IS RECYCLED INTO... PAPER!

1 The paper, sorted by colour and type, is soaked in a tank of water and chemicals to separate the fibres.

2 The mixture is filtered to remove paper clips, labels, staples and tape.

4 The pulp (99 per cent water, 1 per cent fibre) is sprayed on to a fast-moving mesh.

3 A cone-shaped container spins the pulp to clean it. Chemicals may be added to help remove old ink.

5 Rollers press water from the paper, which is then fed through more, heated, rollers for drying and smoothing. Wound on to rolls, the paper is ready to be transported for cutting or printing elsewhere.

DON'T FLUSH TREES DOWN THE LOO – LOOK OUT FOR TOILET PAPER MADE FROM RECYCLED PAPER!

Cardboard is brown because it is unbleached (wood pulp is naturally brown). It's often made with pulp from recycled paper. Cardboard must be separated from paper before recycling to stop brown flecks appearing in the new paper product.

WHAT YOU CAN DO

Find out if you need to separate paper and cardboard in your area.

✔ Do the scrunch test – if the paper remains scrunched, it can be recycled. Non-recyclable paper, with metal or plastic films, springs back into shape.

✔ Remove any sticky tape.

✔ Try to keep paper clean – grease and liquids may mean it can't be recycled.

✔ Greaseproof paper, baking paper, tissues, wet wipes or used paper towels can't be recycled – neither can paper with paint on it.

PERFECT PAPER

When you reuse and recycle, you help to save the planet — and you might save some pennies, too! Why buy something new? Be crafty with old paper around your home.

REDUCE AND REUSE

There are lots of things you can do to reduce paper usage and make the most of the paper you have.

 Use your own cup for takeaway drinks. Some cafés offer a discount when you bring your own.

 Try not to print things out — read on screen instead.

Old school exercise books make great notepads and doodle books! Use their covers to make greeting cards or gift tags.

Bring your own lunch box to the takeaway sandwich or fish and chip shop.

 Donate old books to charity shops or to your school.

PAPER PRODUCTS CAN ONLY BE RECYCLED ABOUT SEVEN TIMES.

DIY UPCYCLING!

Ask your family if they have old wallpaper, maps, boxes or books too tatty to be donated. Then get cutting, sticking, colouring and folding!

WRAPPING PAPER

Use pages from magazines or newspapers.

PARTY PAPERCHAIN

Glue or tape paper strips to link loops.

! Ask an adult to help you with any cutting.

CUP COASTER

Fold up strips of magazine paper and glue them in a coil.

ORIGAMI ANIMAL

Fold up scraps of paper.

PAPIER-MACHÉ MODEL

Mix flour and water to make glue to hold it together.

TRY TO CRAFT WITH BITS AND PIECES THAT CAN'T GO IN YOUR RECYCLING BIN.

ARE YOU A PAPER PRO?
Test your knowledge...

1. Which of these can be renewable?

- **A.** Oil
- **B.** Coal
- **C.** Wood

2. Paper pulp is...

- **A.** Crushed-up coal
- **B.** Mushed-up wood fibres
- **C.** Mashed-up potato

3. Paper can be recycled...

- **A.** 1 to 2 times
- **B.** About 7 times
- **C.** Endlessly

Answers are at the back of the book.

METAL

Have you picked up a steel knife and fork today, pedalled an aluminium bike or swung open an iron gate? Metal is all around us, but sometimes you won't see it. Precious metals are hidden inside unexpected places.

FOR EVERY MILLION MOBILE PHONES RECYCLED, WE CAN EXTRACT 34 KG OF GOLD, 350 KG OF SILVER AND 16 TONNES OF COPPER!

GOLDEN GADGETS

Anything that has a battery or is plugged into a socket uses electricity. Gold conducts electricity (allows it to flow through) better than almost any other material. It can be easily moulded into different shapes, and it doesn't rust. Gold is painted on to the green circuit boards that are the brains of computers, phones, televisions and other electronics.

GOLD-MINING

Gold comes from ore – rocks that contain small amounts of metal. The gold ore is drilled or blasted from mines, then the gold is extracted using crushers and chemicals. It's much easier and greener to get gold from e-waste (old electronic and electrical equipment). Up to 800 times more gold can be extracted from one tonne of recycled circuit boards than from one tonne of gold ore.

MAKING METAL

Metal is a type of mineral, a material that forms naturally in rocks over millions of years. Metals are often strong, shiny and able to conduct heat or electricity – perfect for making cars, jewellery, cooking pans and electronics.

STEELWORKS

Steel is the most widely used metal in the world. It's made from iron ore, which is melted inside a superhot, energy-gulping blast furnace.

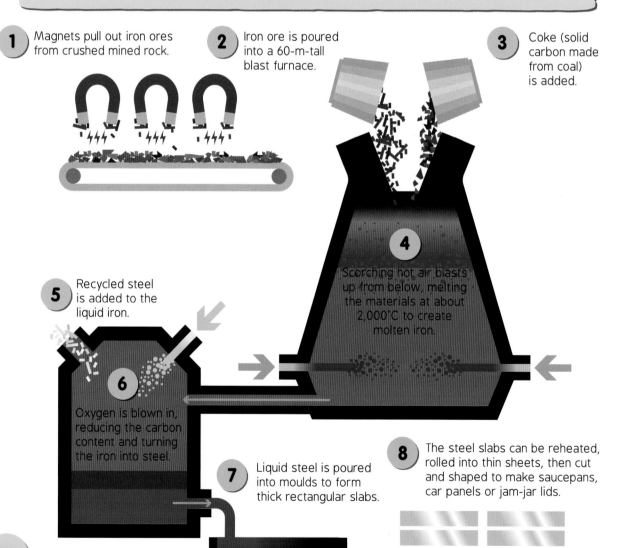

1 Magnets pull out iron ores from crushed mined rock.

2 Iron ore is poured into a 60-m-tall blast furnace.

3 Coke (solid carbon made from coal) is added.

4 Scorching hot air blasts up from below, melting the materials at about 2,000°C to create molten iron.

5 Recycled steel is added to the liquid iron.

6 Oxygen is blown in, reducing the carbon content and turning the iron into steel.

7 Liquid steel is poured into moulds to form thick rectangular slabs.

8 The steel slabs can be reheated, rolled into thin sheets, then cut and shaped to make saucepans, car panels or jam-jar lids.

EVERY YEAR, MINES AND FACTORIES PRODUCE 13 BILLION TONNES OF CO_2. ABOUT ONE-QUARTER OF THIS COMES FROM STEEL- AND IRON-MAKING.

FOSSIL FUELS

Steel-making uses coke made from coal. Coal is also burnt inside power stations to make electricity for mines and steelworks. Like oil and gas, coal is a fossil fuel, formed over millions of years from the fossils of animals buried underground. When it is burnt, coal releases planet-warming CO_2 and toxic gases.

In many places, the steel-making industry is trying to clean up its act by using less coal and coke. Using scrap steel in the process requires up to 60 per cent less energy because there's no need for a blast furnace.

TOTALLY **TRUE** - OR - FOOLISHLY **FALSE?**

☐ Blast furnaces are supercool refrigerators that freeze iron.

☐ Metals, like fossil fuels, are non-renewable (not easily replaced or grown again).

Answers are at the back of the book.

RECYCLING METAL

The mining and processing of metals harms our planet, but it's not all bad news. Like glass, metal can be recycled endlessly. Making a can from recycled metal uses a whopping 95 per cent less energy than from new metal.

HOW A DRINK CAN IS RECYCLED INTO A... DRINK CAN!

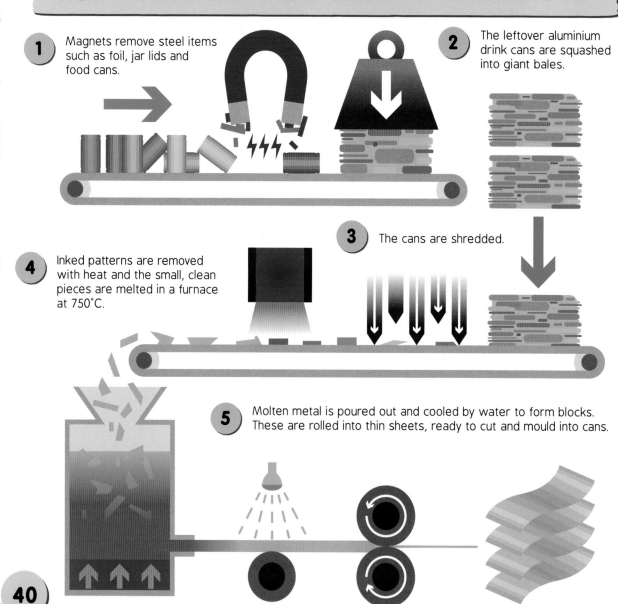

1 Magnets remove steel items such as foil, jar lids and food cans.

2 The leftover aluminium drink cans are squashed into giant bales.

3 The cans are shredded.

4 Inked patterns are removed with heat and the small, clean pieces are melted in a furnace at 750°C.

5 Molten metal is poured out and cooled by water to form blocks. These are rolled into thin sheets, ready to cut and mould into cans.

WHAT YOU CAN DO!

There are lots of things you can do to help cut down metal waste.

✓ Food and drinks cans, and aerosols (spray cans), can all go in your recycling bin.

✓ Ask an adult to help you find out where to recycle e-waste.

✓ Dismantle broken toys to extract any metal.

✓ Make a piggybank for small bits of scrap metal. When it's full, empty it in the metal skip at your local dump.

✓ Leave metal lids on glass bottles and jars, and recycle them with your glass. They'll be extracted and recycled separately.

✓ Squash together foil sheets and containers – larger chunks are easier to recycle.

✓ Scrunch-test your foil! If it springs back into shape, it's not foil but plastic with a thin layer of metal. This material, used for crisp packets, can't go in your recycling bin. It needs specialist recycling.

✓ Batteries must not go in landfill – they leak toxic metals such as lead and mercury, which poison soil and water. Ask an adult to remove and recycle them separately.

IN 2005, A TWO-TONNE BRONZE SCULPTURE BY HENRY MOORE WAS STOLEN AND MELTED DOWN FOR SCRAP. THE SCULPTURE WAS WORTH £3 MILLION; THE SCRAP ONLY £1,500!

METAL MARVELS

Remember how difficult it is to make steel from rocks? Those metal-rich ores will one day run out. We need to think of all metal as precious, not just the gold and silver that wraps around fingers and dangles from ears. Use (and reuse) it wisely – and have some fun with it!

REDUCE AND REUSE

Making, and even recycling, metal is a polluting process, so reduce your use. Challenge yourself to keep single-use metal (that's foil!) out of the kitchen.

✓ Say no to foil takeaway containers – take your own tubs!

✓ Take your old kettle or toaster to a repair shop for fixing rather than throwing them away.

✓ If you do use foil, wipe it clean and reuse it.

✓ Don't wrap your sandwiches in foil – use a lunch box or a reusable covering.

✓ Donate or sell working e-waste.

✓ Rechargeable batteries will help you reduce battery use.

✓ Give old mobile phones to charity shops – they often raise money by sending off phones for recycling. Be sure to wipe any data first.

DIY UPCYCLING!

Make a marvellous metal model! When you've finished with your masterpiece, dismantle it and recycle.

PLANT POT

Decorate it with bits and bobs from around your home.

STAPLE SCULPTURE

Stack old, bent staples or paper clips on an upturned fridge magnet.

ETCH A PICTURE

Use the rounded end of a pen lid or paintbrush to draw on to foil!

CUTLERY CLOCK

Paint the cutlery crazy colours!

ARE YOU A MASTER OF METALS?

Test your knowledge...

1. Where does metal come from?

☐ **A.** Magnets

☐ **B.** Coal

☐ **C.** Rocks called ores

2. Which metal do we use the most?

☐ **A.** Steel

☐ **B.** Gold

☐ **C.** Aluminium

3. Steel-making factories release...

☐ **A.** Carbon dioxide

☐ **B.** Carbon monoxide

☐ **C.** Both these gases

Answers are at the back of the book.

CLOTH

Billowing sheets of cloth in a rainbow of colours are cut up and stitched together to make trousers, towels and curtains. Cloth can be made from plastic fibres or natural fibres, such as silk or sheep's wool. The most common natural fabric of all is cotton, which begins life in a field.

FIELD TO FABRIC

Cotton is a plant with a hard seed case that pops open to reveal a ball of soft, white, fluffy fibres. The fibres are harvested and spun into thread to make cloth. Cotton is grown as a crop in warm parts of the world. As our climate changes, these areas suffer from more and more floods and droughts, which devastate the cotton fields.

FARM NOT HARM

Cotton farming often uses polluting chemicals and huge amounts of water, sucking rivers and wells dry and depriving people of essential supplies. But some farmers are learning how to use less water and how to make pesticides from plants. They hope to save money, water and the planet!

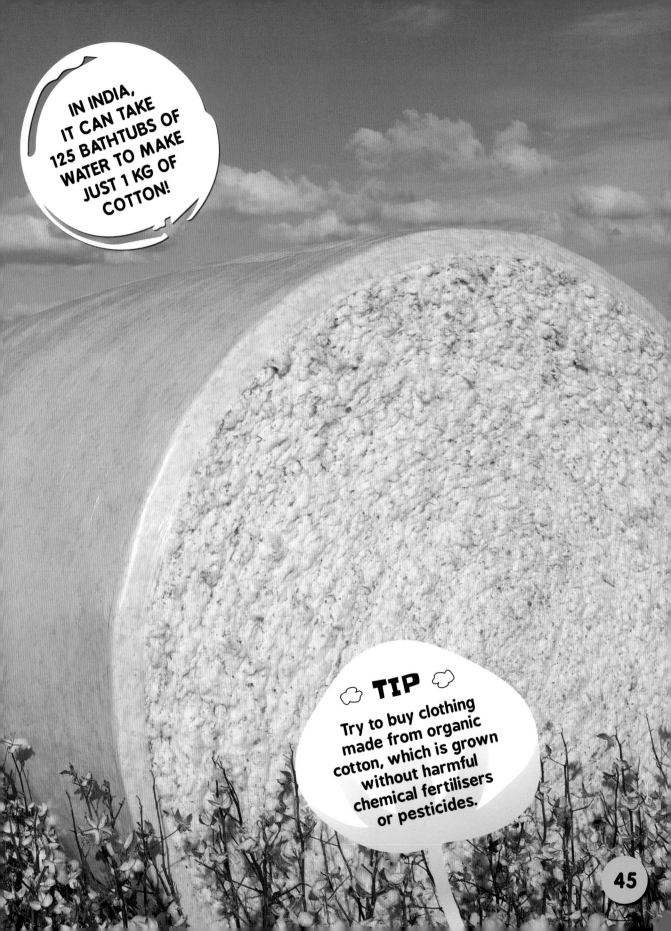

IN INDIA, IT CAN TAKE 125 BATHTUBS OF WATER TO MAKE JUST 1 KG OF COTTON!

TIP

Try to buy clothing made from organic cotton, which is grown without harmful chemical fertilisers or pesticides.

MAKING CLOTH

How many fabrics are you wearing right now? A woolly jumper, polyester trousers, or pants with stretchy plastic elastic? You might well be wearing a cotton T-shirt. Let's find out how that's made...

COTTON MILL

It takes about 48 hours for raw cotton to be cleaned, combed and stretched into a thin cotton thread.

1 Raw cotton, harvested by hand or machine from fields, arrives at the mill in huge bales.

2 The cotton is broken apart and blown about to remove any leaves and twigs.

3 Seeds are also separated – they will be used for animal feed.

5 A coiler curls out a thick rope of cotton, called sliver.

4 A carding machine combs the cotton with huge toothed rollers. This untangles the fibres and lines them up in rows.

7 The cotton thread is wound on to spools.

6 The sliver is twisted and stretched over rollers into strong, thin threads.

8 The threads feed into a loom, which weaves them into a sheet of fabric, ready to be cut and sewn into a T-shirt.

CHECK THE LABEL TO SEE WHAT YOUR CLOTHES ARE MADE OF.

ROT OR NOT?

Your cotton T-shirt would take about five months to biodegrade. A woolly hat could take one year and a silk tie could take several years. Your polyester fleece, however, would take hundreds of years to biodegrade!

COTTON IS RENEWABLE, BUT EVERY YEAR THE CLOTH INDUSTRY USES 98 MILLION TONNES OF NON-RENEWABLE RESOURCES, INCLUDING OIL, TO MAKE A SYNTHETIC (MAN-MADE) FABRIC CALLED POLYESTER.

In the USA and many other countries, banknotes are made with cotton, not paper. Some banknotes are coated in a plastic polymer film and have the lowest lifetime carbon footprint. They last much longer than paper or cotton ones, so less energy and materials are needed to reprint new notes.

TOTALLY TRUE - OR - FOOLISHLY FALSE?

Two-thirds of all the materials used in the cloth industry are made from plastics.

A polyester fleece is made from sheep's wool.

Answers are at the back of the book.

RECYCLING CLOTH

All cloth, even old rags that your dog has chewed, should be recycled. Natural cotton fibres can be spun into new thread, and polyester clothes can be shredded to make stuffing for sofas and car seats.

HOW A T-SHIRT IS RECYCLED INTO... A T-SHIRT!

1 Clothes that can be reused are picked out and sent to charities that can sell them.

2 The remaining clothes are sorted by fabric type and by colour (so no re-dyeing is needed later).

3 The fabrics are chopped and shredded again and again.

4 Fluffy cotton scraps are carded into fibres, and some new cotton is added. Sliver is coiled out and spun into thread.

5 Plastic-based shredded scraps are compressed to make thick pads of insulation and filling for mattresses, car seats and sofas.

48

Shoes can be recycled, too. Rubber trainer soles can be transformed into springy playground surfaces. Trainers can also be made from recycled car tyres and plastic bottles.

EACH SECOND, ONE RUBBISH TRUCK FULL OF TEXTILES (CLOTH AND CLOTHING) IS DUMPED IN A LANDFILL OR BURNT.

RECYCLING TIPS

Here are some things to remember to help you recycle clothes and other cloth items.

 Fabrics must be washed before recycling.

 Tie pairs of shoes together.

 Collect arts and crafts materials – save buttons, zips, lace or frills from clothing that can't be re-worn.

 To keep them clean and dry, bag your clothes before you tip them in the bank.

RAGS TO RICHES

Is your wardrobe full of clothes you don't wear? Ignore fast fashion — only buy clothes you need, and wear them until they're too small or they fall apart. Then upcycle your rags into funky new things.

REDUCE AND REUSE

Remember — reducing is always better than reusing and recycling. So try to buy fewer clothes, especially ones made of polyester, nylon and other plastics.

✔ Donate good-quality clothes to charity.

✔ Repair your clothes — knee patches make your jeans last longer!

✔ Search charity shops for unusual items.

✔ Use old rags for wiping and dusting.

✔ Host a clothes-swap party.

✔ Store marbles, game-board pieces and other bits and bobs in an old sock.

GLOBALLY, WE COULD SAVE £360 BILLION BY REUSING CLOTHES INSTEAD OF BUYING NEW ONES.

DIY UPCYCLING!

You're growing fast, but you don't need to say goodbye to all your old clothes. Transform them with scissors, sewing and sequins!

RAG RUG

Tie together twisted strips of rags.

T-SHIRT TRICKS

Frame it or make a cushion cover!

! Ask an adult to help you with any sewing — needles are sharp!

SOCK PUPPET

Sew on buttons for eyes and wool for hair.

RAG BAG

Cut a fringe along the bottom and tie the strips together, then turn inside out.

ARE YOU CLUED UP ABOUT CLOTH?

Test your knowledge...

1. Which of these are not made with natural fibres?

- **A.** Cotton T-shirt
- **B.** Silk shirt
- **C.** Polyester trousers

2. What do you call the thick rope of cotton coiled out at the mill?

- **A.** Silver
- **B.** Sliver
- **C.** Saliva

3. Which banknote material saves the most carbon?

- **A.** Plastic
- **B.** Cotton
- **C.** Silk

Answers are at the back of the book.

FOOD

Surely a simple sandwich isn't bad for the environment? We all have to eat – food is important and enjoyable – but we need to think about how our food is made, packaged and transported. Let's investigate the carbon footprint of a cheese-and-ham sandwich.

FOOD FROM THE FARM

A cheese-and-ham sandwich produces 1,350 g of CO_2 – that's the same as driving a car 18 km! It takes lots of energy to farm animals, so the animal products in your sandwich have a higher carbon footprint than the bread or any vegetables you might include. Farm animals also need land to live on, and more land is needed to grow the crops they eat.

IF A FIELD THE SIZE OF A FOOTBALL PITCH WAS FARMED WITH ANIMALS FOR MILK, EGGS AND MEAT, IT COULD FEED FIVE TO TEN PEOPLE FOR ONE YEAR. THE SAME FIELD COULD GROW ENOUGH FRUIT, VEGETABLES AND GRAIN CROPS TO FEED UP TO 30 PEOPLE FOR A YEAR.

KEEPING COOL

Sandwiches, wrapped in paper and plastic, are transported in fuel-guzzling refrigerated trucks. At the supermarket or café, they sit inside refrigerated cabinets that gobble up electricity. All this adds to the carbon footprint.

A HOME-MADE SANDWICH USES ABOUT HALF THE CARBON OF THE SAME SANDWICH BOUGHT IN A SHOP.

As grass digests in their stomachs, cows produce the powerful greenhouse gas methane. Cows burp billions of tonnes of methane every year, but mixing seaweed into their food could reduce this by as much as 99 per cent!

MAKING FOOD

When food is processed inside a factory, some weird and not-so-wonderful ingredients may be added. Read the labels on packets. Think about how and where your food was grown, the machinery used, and how it was transported.

FOOD FACTORY

To stop food rotting on the shelf it's frozen or preservatives are added.

1 Fish is packed into containers and frozen into blocks.

2 The blocks are sliced into strips.

4 The fish fingers are coated in breadcrumbs.

3 The strips are dipped in batter made with flour.

5 Then flash fried.

6 Then frozen with a blast of icy liquid nitrogen.

8 The boxes are stacked inside refrigerated trucks and sent off to the supermarket.

7 The fish fingers are dropped into plastic liners, then card boxes.

⚓ TIP ⚓

Overfishing can wipe out fish populations, and sometimes dolphins, whales and turtles are accidentally caught up in the nets. Buy seafood marked 'sustainable', which means that wildlife and natural habitats have been looked after.

WHAT IS ORGANIC FOOD?

Organic food is made without using harmful chemicals to feed animals or spray crops. Chemicals that kill crop-eating insects also kill bees, which fertilise wildflowers and are very important for our natural spaces. The chemicals also sink into soil and wash into rivers, spreading the toxic damage.

THE PALM OIL PROBLEM

When rainforests are cleared to plant palm trees for oil production, animals like orang-utans lose their homes. But palm oil can have a low carbon footprint – it needs less than half the land that other crops need to produce the same amount of oil. Look for sustainable palm oil, which doesn't harm natural habitats.

TOTALLY TRUE - OR - FOOLISHLY FALSE?

☐ Cows burp the greenhouse gas oxygen.

☐ You can lower your carbon footprint by eating less meat.

Answers are at the back of the book.

RECYCLING FOOD

Food decomposes easily, so why not just chuck leftovers in the bin? The problem is that pesky gas methane — huge amounts are released when food rots in an oxygen-deprived landfill. But recycled food can be made into garden compost, farm fertilisers and even electricity.

HOW FOOD WASTE IS RECYCLED INTO... ELECTRICITY!

1 Food waste is poured into a tightly sealed, oxygen-free tank.

3 As the waste rots, it gives off biogas, which is collected in a huge storage unit.

2 Tiny organisms break down the food in a process called 'anaerobic digestion'.

4 The waste turns into a sludgy wet mush that can be used as a fertiliser on farms.

5 The gas is piped to homes for cooking and heating water, or to a generator to be converted into electricity.

EVERY YEAR, WE THROW AWAY ABOUT ONE THIRD OF OUR FOOD – THAT'S 1.3 BILLION TONNES OF ROTTING WASTE, PUMPING OUT 3.3 BILLION TONNES OF GREENHOUSE GASES!

RECYCLING JUST ONE LORRYLOAD OF FOOD WASTE CAN MAKE ENOUGH ENERGY TO POWER 20,000 TVS FOR ONE HOUR!

COOL COMPOST

Unlike landfill, compost heaps contain oxygen, so no methane is created in compost. If you can, compost garden waste and uncooked food waste. Add toilet rolls and egg boxes for carbon, but not meat or fish. Within 9 to 12 months, you'll have a rich compost for your plants!

RECYCLING TIPS

Find out if your area collects food waste.

 Get a kitchen caddy, a tub or small bin with a lid. Line it with newspaper or a biodegradable bag.

 Empty all leftover food into the bin, even raw or cooked meat.

 Keep the caddy out of sunlight to stop waste rotting and smelling too quickly.

 Make sure there is no packaging mixed in with the food.

 Pour liquids down the sink – not into the caddy.

FOOD FUN

Now you know about food's carbon footprint and the effort it takes to recycle it, perhaps you'll lick your dinner plate clean! The aim of the game is to scrape as little as possible into your trash or recycling bin. Some food (and garden) waste can even be awesomely upcycled!

REDUCE AND REUSE

To reduce waste (and save money), buy only what you need. Think about food packaging — can you reduce that, too?

✔ Over-ripe bananas can be blended into smoothies or milkshakes.

✔ Sprinkle stale breadcrumbs on puddings or home-made fishcakes.

✔ Put leftovers in the fridge or freezer, not the bin.

✔ Choose food with less or recyclable packaging.

✔ Reduce your meat — munch on barbecue-flavoured crickets for a protein-rich sustainable snack!

☼ TIP ☼
Up to 40 per cent of vegetables are thrown away because some supermarkets don't like the way they look. Seek out wonky fruit and veg — they taste just as good!

DIY UPCYCLING!

What can you whisk away from your food or garden bins to bring back to life?

BIRD FEEDER

Press seeds and leftover fat into a shell or tin.

WORMERY

Compostable waste makes great worm food!

PEPPER PLANT

Plant pepper seeds in a pot on a sunny windowsill.

GET STICKY

Frame a favourite photo with sticks.

! Steer clear of old meat and dairy products or anything mouldy — they could make you sick.

ARE YOU FILLED IN ABOUT FOOD?
Test your knowledge...

1. Which food has the lowest carbon footprint?

 A. Cheese

 B. Ham

 C. Carrot

2. Which word describes food farmed without harmful chemicals?

A. Processed

B. Anaerobic

C. Organic

3. How much food do we throw away each year?

 A. One half

 B. One third

 C. One quarter

Answers are at the back of the book.

THE FUTURE IS GREEN

The planet is under threat from our troublesome trash, but scientists are working hard to solve the problem. Some ideas are sensible; others weird and wacky. But don't forget, YOU now have the knowledge to face the future and paint it green.

NATURE'S INCINERATORS?

Why not blast our rubbish into the Sun? To launch just one dustbin full of trash into orbit would cost more than £450,000 – and then think of the fuel bill to complete the 150-million-km journey to the Sun! Or how about chucking trash into volcanoes? They would overflow and belch out horrible trashy fumes, and they're not hot enough to melt metals likes iron and titanium.

GREAT DEGRADABLES

Reducing packaging is the greenest option of all, but look out for biodegradable plant-based materials: soaps wrapped in rice paper; plastic-like bags and food boxes made with corn; a mushroom-and-oat recipe to replace the polystyrene packaging inside boxes. You can even dress top-to-toe in a fabric made from pineapple!

FIVE WAYS TO BE A GREEN SUPERHERO!
Wear an invisible green cape everyday and get to work!

✓ Volunteer to be your class recycling monitor.

✓ Go green for gifts – make presents, wrapping paper and cards from old stuff.

✓ Join a park or beach clean-up.

✓ Write a letter full of green ideas to the government.

✓ Save energy and water – turn off taps and lights.

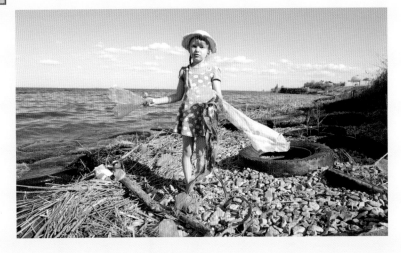

✗ TIP ✗
Some poorer countries do not have good waste and recycling systems. Check out wasteaid.org. This charity helps people cope with and earn a living from their rubbish, collecting biogas from food scraps or building a school with plastic bottles.

GLOSSARY

ACID RAIN
Rain that contains acid formed from factory gases such as sulphur dioxide. Acid rain pollutes Earth's water and soil, kills animals and wears away metals and stone.

BIODEGRADABLE
Able to rot away into tiny pieces of natural material, helped by natural processes involving bacteria and fungi.

CARBON
A substance that can be found naturally as a diamond or a soft grey-black rock called graphite. Most commonly, carbon mixes with other substances to form new substances, such as the gas carbon dioxide.

CARBON DIOXIDE (CO$_2$)
A colourless, odourless gas released when fossil fuels such as coal, oil and gas are burnt. Volcanoes produce CO$_2$, and animals and humans breathe it out.

CARBON FOOTPRINT
The amount of carbon dioxide and other greenhouse gases that an object or activity produces during its whole 'lifetime'.

CHEMICAL
A substance with a certain group of characteristics. Natural chemicals include gold and salt. Synthetic chemicals are made by people and mixed together to form new substances. Some of these, such as toxic pesticides, can harm the environment.

CLIMATE CHANGE
The changing of weather patterns and the warming of Earth over a long period of time.

DECOMPOSE
To break down into small pieces or rot away.

DEGRADE
To get worse, often in strength, usability or appearance.

ENERGY
The power from electricity or fossil fuels that provides heat or makes machines move.

ENVIRONMENT
Our natural surroundings, including plants, forests, deserts, oceans and the air we breathe. Animals, weather and Earth's climate are also part of the environment.

E-WASTE
Waste from electronic items, which use batteries or electricity. E-waste includes old ovens, televisions and mobile phones.

FERTILISER
A substance added to soil to help plants grow.

FIBRE
A small, thin, thread-like strand.

FOSSIL FUEL
Natural oil, gas or coal, which formed underground millions of years ago from decomposing plants and animals. Fossil fuels contain a large amount of carbon.

GREENHOUSE GAS
A gas such as carbon dioxide or methane that wraps around our planet, keeping it warm. The gases create the same effect as a greenhouse – they let heat in but not out.

INCINERATE
To destroy something by burning.

LANDFILL
An area or pit where non-recyclable waste is dumped and stored.

METHANE
A powerful greenhouse gas produced when plant matter decomposes with no oxygen present. Natural gas is mostly methane.

MICROBEADS
Tiny round pieces of plastic sometimes used in shower gel to scrub away dirt. Biodegradable alternatives include ground-up walnut shells.

MICROFIBRES
Tiny plastic fibres that make up plastic-based fabrics such as polyester and nylon.

MICROPLASTIC
Very small (often microscopic) pieces of plastic.

NATURAL RESOURCES
Useful materials, such as wood, coal and water, that occur naturally on Earth.

ORE
A rock from which metal can be extracted.

ORGANIC
Describing a process that is carried out, or a product that is made, without the use of harmful chemicals. (Organic can also mean 'made from living things'.)

OXYGEN
A colourless, odourless gas, mainly produced by plants. Animals and plants need oxygen to live.

PESTICIDE
A substance sprayed onto crops to kill weeds, plant diseases and crop-eating insects.

POLLUTE
To add substances that cause harm, often with chemicals toxic to living things.

POLYESTER
Cloth made from plastic fibres.

RECYCLE
To turn old waste into new objects. The waste is broken up, cleaned, heated or melted to create new materials.

RENEWABLE
Never runs out or is easily replaced. Renewable natural resources include water, air and carefully managed timber forests. Non-renewable resources include oil, coal and gas.

REUSABLE
Able to be used again and again.

SINGLE-USE
Used only once before being recycled or thrown away. Packaging is often single-use.

SUSTAINABLE
Describing a process that is carried out, or a product that is made, without long-term harm to plants, animals or their natural habitats. Sustainability also means that local farmers and factory workers are paid fairly and less pollution is produced.

TOXIC
Poisonous and likely to cause harm to plants or animals.

UPCYCLE
To repair, decorate or change an object to transform it into something new.

ANSWERS

PAGE 15
PLASTIC: TOTALLY TRUE OR FOOLISHLY FALSE?
True: Up to 700,000 plastic microfibres are released from polyester or nylon clothes during a single washing cycle.

The second fact is false.

PAGE 19
ARE YOU A PROFESSOR OF PLASTICS?
1C, 2B, 3A

PAGE 23
GLASS: TOTALLY TRUE OR FOOLISHLY FALSE?
True: Some sand is mined illegally – sand thieves have stolen an entire beach in a single night!

The second fact is false.

PAGE 27
ARE YOU A GLASS GEEK?
1B, 2A, 3C

PAGE 31
PAPER: TOTALLY TRUE OR FOOLISHLY FALSE?
True: Sulphur dioxide is often released from paper factories, causing acid rain.

The second fact is false.

PAGE 35
ARE YOU A PAPER PRO?
1C, 2B, 3B

PAGE 39
METAL: TOTALLY TRUE OR FOOLISHLY FALSE?
The first fact is false.

True: Metals, like fossil fuels, are non-renewable (not easily replaced or grown again).

PAGE 43
ARE YOU A MASTER OF METALS?
1C, 2A, 3C

PAGE 47
CLOTH: TOTALLY TRUE OR FOOLISHLY FALSE?
True: Two-thirds of all the materials used in the cloth industry are made from plastics.

The second fact is false.

PAGE 51
ARE YOU CLUED UP ABOUT CLOTH?
1C, 2B, 3A

PAGE 55
FOOD: TOTALLY TRUE OR FOOLISHLY FALSE?
The first fact is false.

True: You can lower your carbon footprint by eating less meat.

PAGE 59
ARE YOU FILLED IN ABOUT FOOD?
1C, 2C, 3B

FIND OUT MORE
Check out **recyclenow.com** for top tips about how to recycle all those tricky bits and pieces. Play games and get crafting at **wastebuster.co.uk**, then explore NASA's awesome website: **climatekids.nasa.gov**